Blue Hunger

Blue Hunger

Poems by
Subhaga Crystal Bacon

ରଓ

Methow Press
Twisp, Washington 98556

© 2020 Subhaga Crystal Bacon

Published by Methow Press

P.O. Box 1213, Twisp, WA 98556
https://www.methowpress.com

Printed in the United States of America

All rights reserved. No part of this publication may be reproduced, stored in a retrieval system, or transmitted in any form or by any means—for example, electronic, photocopy or recording—without the prior written permission of the publisher. The only exception is brief quotations in printed reviews.

ISBN 13: 978-0-9787554-9-2

Cover image © Sugandhi Katharine Barnes. Used by permission.
Cover graphics design by Greg Wright.

for Sugandhi
and the Trillium Awakening Community

For dna & Lisa with love and friendship!

XO

Crystal

Contents

Invitation	3
Intimacies	
When I Watch You	7
On Reading Stafford	8
Altar	9
My Mother's Laundry	10
Pealing	11
Memento Mori	12
Joined Here Together	13
On a Morning Like This	14
Finding Home	15
Nights Without You	16
August Gift	17
Accretion of Hope	18
Compelled	19
When You Hold Me That Way	20
Clean	21
Wild Emergence	22
Outside at the woodpile	23
On a Saturday Morning	24
Years: A Koan	25
Weekend in Human Life	26
Long and Lengthening: Sweet, Dark Season	27
Summing It All Up	28
Walking the Familiar	29

Margaret's Heart	30
Awake at Night	32
My Soul is a Candle That Burned Away the Veil	33

Melancholy

Lament for Oso, Washington	37
Ed's Fence	38
Song	40
Paradise, Lost	41
What I Know of Melancholy	43
Spill	44
The Weight of Grief	45
November Morning	46
Always Forgetting the Little Things	47
March Journal	48
Wound	49
Sounding	50
Lost Boys	51

Quirks

Blue Hunger	55
A Sign on the Cascade Highway	56
With Time	57
Waiting	58
Limbs of Love	59
Morning Quail	60
Feeling the Falling	61
At Home on the Range	62
Emptiness Disguised	63
Now I Lay Me Down	64
Quirks of Nature	65
Fear	66
Soundscape	68
Coyotes Sing When They Kill	69
Beauty Broken Whole	70
Uprising	71
Picking Raspberries	72

The Time Between Wolf and Dog	73
Country Life	74
After the Solstice	75
She Writes in Light	76
My Mother's Hands	77
Girl Meets Boy	78
Night Walk	79
City of Embers	80
Mundane	81
Acknowledgments	83
About the Author	85

*the landscape, like a verse in the psalter,
is weight and ardor and eternity.*

> Rainer Maria Rilke, "The Man Watching"

What more can any of us ask for but to be created by the very thing we feel compelled to create?

> Mark Nepo, *The River of Light*

Invitation

When you are ready,
come. I will be waiting
by the river's
purling hurry,
slim or sleek
with spring.
We will walk there
and your story—
river in ice,
river hurling—
will quicken
our two hearts
nodding, knotted
in knowing.
When you are ready,
I will be waiting.
Green as daylight
rich in wonder.

I will be rain
to your thunder.

☙❧

Intimacies

When I Watch You

after Lucille Clifton

The years collapse
like so many leaves
in a book. In the morning
fresh from your soak
and shower, your fragrance
     slips into the collage
of cinnamon and grains
like the scent of a secret
garden. Your long bones,
legs, arms, neck, hold
and are held by you.
You become absorbed
by what you do: eating,
drinking, reading. We
orbit each other like twin
moons on an elliptic around
a mysterious gravitational pull,
planet or star, shedding light
and shadow like notes
in some celestial symphony.
When I watch you, really
watch you, I don't see
     you at all. I feel
the slender, tensile filament
that holds us in space.

        ଓଛୋ

On Reading Stafford's "Is This Feeling about the West Real"

The gunpowder green tea unfurls
its hand-rolled pearls, fragrant
in the stoneware pot by the sink,
mixed with local honey in my cup,
too hot to drink. The steam curls up.
There's a book, and the sun-warm
kitchen nook where I camp out,
a vagrant, on days off from work,
longing to linger for hours.

But something wild—beyond the dog
impatient at my feet—tugs at me
to go outside where brown hills
of golden grass roll off to places unseen.

Walking, climbing the hardscrabble
to go the way the deer have trod,
I reach this primal air that twists trees
into hunched shapes mythical as gods
that show how hard—how vital it is
to bend. Blocks of sedimentary rock,
one-time islands of ancient seas,
crop up as steppes and ledges to rest upon.

West, and further west, the ageless peaks
break the sky or disappear behind fog.
White with new snow or old, or gray
as pencil lead, they draw me over land
on my fragile human legs, blown-open,
full of hunger for their silent knowing—
more real, more ancient than marks on clay,
or page—literal only to the heart.

Altar

Rock rises from the autumn grass
and golden blossoms dry as the land
that birthed them. Lichen points upward,
arrow-shaped invitation.
I sprawl backward in its embrace
face turned up to November's blue,
waning moon slowly setting
in the west. *Tok tok tok*
the raven's call sounds out the distances.
Across the river, smoke drifts
white down-valley. Amid the burnt
posts and bitterbrush marking old
fire, a clearing and burning for safety.

Rise. Cleft. Bowl. Outcrop. Perch
in the endless fold of hills almost flat
against the meeting sky. Ravens close
above, their wing beats like breaths.
Curious, they circle until hawk reveals
his white under-feathers. They dance
in air like the first people who swooped,
winged and beaded in honor of what flies.

I could lie here in these boulder arms
until snow comes to cover my naked bones.
Hawk hovers over raven to catch at flesh.
Death feeds what lives, its hunger
appeased, rises like moon, like life
burning and consuming before it falls.

ଓଃଓ

My Mother's Laundry

Shifting wet clothes from washer to dryer
to basket for hanging, I remember my mother's words.
If I were a single career woman, she would begin,
*I would just hand-wash my bras and panties
at night*, as she washed, dried, and ironed for five.

What I recall most was the flavor of those words,
scented with lost possibilities, sweet
and delicate as meringues. Our basement with its asbestos
tiles in coffee and cream, the heater humming
while it worked, cement walls, and the door
to the finished room with its knotty pine—
so many textures to dream upon.

So much of my life was lived beneath the house:
on the cool floor, cutting fabric patterns,
the sewing machine's light. And at night,
those college years, the TV and couches,
doing homework to Johnny Carson and black
and white movies that merged with the words I sorted,
scoured, and pressed, in notebooks for poems:
    inchoate, caritas, anima.
My dreams of love and freedom freighted under
all that weighed us down in the suburbs of our lives.

    ☙

Pealing

Slicing through softening snow,
February, after Imbolc, the midpoint
between winter and spring. Out of milky
sky, a song penetrates me, skin to bone.
Bald eagle soars up over the ditch,
white trees—cottonwood, aspen—
fire-dead five years.
      Eagle song
runs like liquid, the lilting peal
that signals danger in their midst.
A warning I hear as music. Earth-
bound. Limited. My arms reach out.
Heart exposed for the taking
follows the white head and tail,
sweeping wings, into the lift.

   ೄ

Memento Mori

Like an ancient sarcophagus of a knight and hound,
we lie on a slab of stone on the breast of a hill.
The view is to the west, place of endings,
quiet and guarded by an anonymous tree,
wind-shaped windbreak. My mind melds
into the expansiveness of cloud, sky, grass,
distant peaks. Everything is foreshortened.
The dark tunnel into trees—just
there—over a mile off, steeply
downhill, across the road and a good walk
to the treeline two properties
away. This is a bench I love above
the house with its walls and roof, doors and windows.
It slopes into a bowl then flattens out,
scattered with rocks and old wood.
I imagine a tarp in the slender branches of tree,
a sleeping bag, and then just myself,
here, facing west, bones on rock,
the cloth of my shoes, fragments aflutter in the waving
grass. My self merged with that great distance,
come close now, because I'm here.

        ☙❧

Joined Here Together

Like us, trees are never alone.
They stand in clusters, or solitary
yet joined to earth and sky. They
reach for eternity, high
and low, a miracle not rent
by tension. No. They simply grow
in opposite directions, down
into dark mysteries of soil
and up to breathe the breath of God.
Like trees, we are bound together:
root, branch, seed.

☙❧

On a Morning Like This

Silence sings
in this bowl
of white
that sweeps up
and out
toward sky.
Not the wind
scouring down
from snow,
carrying northern light,
scent of ice.
The ice itself
is a music, glinting.

And the river.
Flickering under frozen
eddies like a flame.

Lone sentinels
along the ridge
exclaim the song
of wood, pop
in the grate,
summer's rain
in the grain of pine.

ඎඏ

Finding Home

First, like Goldilocks, I must sleep—
not in your bed, but in the night song.
In summer, does the whir of cicadas rupture
silence deep as the moonless night? In spring
the river's rushing roar, and in fall the aspen
leaves' nervous flutter. Then there's the water.
It must come from a well and be neither
too hard nor too soft. Does the soap rinse
clean leaving skin and hair naked as new?
Does it taste like mountain air with a hint
of nothing? Are there birds? Will they hum
and flitter to nectar and branch? Will they eat
the late fall seed emerging from clover? Do
coyotes sing their happy feeding song
over snow, over late summer dawns? And deer.
Do the mules spring gracefully, hooves meeting
in balletic rapture? And raptors. Do they cry
in the high blue day, snakes drooping to the nest?
Home is here. I can rest.

❧

Nights Without You

Nights used to be dark inside,
blue-lit by the TV screen,
and outside dim from streetlights.
I drew the blinds in my solitude
and drank, and watched predator eating prey
with a cool voice behind. Watched
movies in black and white, rich tones
in shades of gray. I used to write at night
staying up late with the wisps of drink
and longing, my empty bed. I used to drive
in the cold nights to the city, skinny
and leather clad, prowling other rooms,
dark and loud with strangers and drumbeats.
I was Clint Eastwood. I was Steve
McQueen with big hair and red lipstick,
waiting at the bar for something,
someone to turn on my lights.

Now, it's light inside, golden with fire.
Shades drawn against the cold
black night, punctured with stars.
It's a long road to anyplace loud.
Night is music, layered and fragrant as wine.
I step out for wood, for radiance, face
upturned like a cup to drink it in,
Venus crossing toward morning, light
bearer. You're away another day.
I'm here, empty of longing.
Luminous, lambent.

೧೩৪೦

August Gift

Over the usual dry silence, the million
soft footsteps, exotic on this desert
summer Sunday. Awakening, my mind reaches
out to cup the din in the cistern of memory.
I unfurl from sleep, from deep fear of fire,
to the smoky grey sky of cloud. Trees
offset in limpid green bow their leaves
to wetness. The earth patters beneath water,
volume increasing in sound and ground.
The overhanging eave built for snow,
where winter's ice melts into spears,
this morning drips with summer's grateful tears.
Runoff returns to river. Reprieve from burn.

ଓଃଡ

Accretion of Hope

after Dickinson

If
something
lands on your
shoulders, think of
that thing with feathers
and song. Feed it from your
open hand, but don't try to
keep it captive. Everything flies
in this life, no matter what. Listen
for its song and look for its flight. It will
return to you wherever you find yourself.

ଓଞ୍ଚ

Compelled

Outside, the snow collapses
on itself, water finding water
that way it has of shifting shape
and staying the same. The river
roars its full-throated runoff,
wicking away what falls.
The arc of light slants higher
across our hills, days longer
by seconds. Still, it's winter.
In this quiet expanse of white-
lit life, we fall into our own
slant of time. Bones resting
on bones that spark in bright
arcs of pain. You paint. I write.
Fire exhales in the grate its long held
breath of rain. Water moving
everywhere, compelled
to start again.

ॐ

When You Hold Me That Way

In the morning, lying in the shell shape
our bodies make curled toward each other,
like a nautilus reversed, my spine unfurls
from the saddle-shaped root where fire
simmers, sends shimmers the length
of the bones. Something flickers, lifts.
Each link drums a message to its kin:
We're awakening. Later in the day,
there's a filigree of gleam over everything
I see, everything I do. In the channel
that holds all the keys to all the locks,
love floods and the boats so sullen
in their muck are once again afloat.

༄༅

Clean

A woman hangs a load of laundry,
like Noah, separating each by purpose,
by type. The wind and sun weave their magic
between the clusters, the fibers, shading dark
to light, wet to dry. Indoors, a screen
flickers another reality. Signals bounce
over mountains and trees, pole to pole,
and falter.

The wind and sun know
no obstacles. They shine and move
by their own wisdom. No one
says, *Go now. Do this; do that.*
Wind sloughs up from river, down
from clouds, snaps jeans and towels, wraps
undergarments thin as skin around
the plastic-coated line, pinches them
on pins.

Looking out over the greening
yard, past the barn toward the rising
hills, pines, then, higher, snow, she reels
in the great open space she shares:
a whole body washed in love.

꘎

Wild Emergence

Today, the foals appeared in fresh-mown
fields, their startled legs akimbo. Spring
snow of apple blossoms accretes street
side, and fresh ditch water paints
plowed fields brown in lilac scented air,
sun warmed after morning's chill.

Around the bend below the last hills
where runoff roils, a doe steps sudden
as shadow into the road. I do not want to kill
what surprises me, this wild emergence.
In the empty lane, I brake and swerve
pitching the staid detritus of my day.
Seeking her on the roadside, I find
only the water-drenched dark of trees.

꧁꧂

Outside at the woodpile

across the sun-bright, snow-drenched field,
birdsong glitters through the frozen air
on flashing wings that scissor light
and land in dark pine cover. Long needles
and supple boughs quiver with life.
All the long winter, they gathered
silent but for the scrabbling of bark
and clatter of pecking millet from the empty
tin base of the feeder. Forlorn rasping.
What joy their sweet notes loft into morning.
Mourning flies like a banner in the shining day.

ଓଃଃ

On a Saturday Morning

Nothing but the ringing in my ear.
And the small tick of fire burning down
to red and white coals in the stove.
I like a second cup of tea in the morning.
Reading. Living fictional lives, dying
their deaths. Hot green tea with honey
that sweetens the tannins and dries my lips.

I'm surrounded by aloneness, this moment
of blood and bones held by skin and clothes,
heart beating and the softness of solitude,
like a wrap of mother's touch. The light is white
fog shrouding the trees flocked and upright
as hair after a shock. Textures. And the small
movements of a pine fingering the invisible air.

          ॐ

Years: A Koan

Nothing is last, nothing first.
Everything is a wheel. Here
and here and here with no room
for there. Even infinity loops
back on itself. While dark,
also bright. Up, also down. Try
to mark what ends from what starts.
Walk on this spinning ball east to west
or north to south, and the place you began
is also moving, like the horizon
out of reach.

Stand still and ride
through the night sky that holds
the morning light. Morning.
The crescent moon hangs
like a comma in the sentence
of your life. Follow it.

☙❧

Weekend in Human Life

Saturday, the dog dislocated her hip.
Today, the vet met an emergency
at the door. A Chihuahua hit by a car
whimpers in the distance, then silent
in its crate going home. My dog
shivers beneath the waiting room bench.

On the road home, sirens. One car,
then another, then the ambulance flashing.
Each time I slow and pull over.
Each delivers a soft blow.

Friends complain about the weight of the world.
The way the body feels living life,
like a sob in the fine lines of nerve
and blood, a crying in the heart.
Everything that lives dies.

Up the bumpy drive to home, the sun
strikes glass like the hammer of God, shatters
me into a thousand tender pieces.

        CO&SO

Long and Lengthening: Sweet, Dark Season

At 6:46 I open the shades to the cold
that washes in clean and bracing
as the river. Six days from Solstice,
the sun still sunken below the horizon,
buried, one story says, in the earth
under the deepening dark
awaiting birth.

Skeletal trees stand guard.

It's not winter yet. A soft snow
the consistency of lard
lingers in the liminal place
between water and ice, gives off
a frozen fog that wraps the air
like a cloak. It's not night. Not quite
light. Everything draped and ghostly.
No fire. No smoke. Just the still,
frozen silence, a kind of blessing,
a kind of peace.

      ଓଞ୍ଚ

Summing It All Up

Sometimes, the light in the morning
up over the newly snowed peaks
breaks open my heart, like a window
hit by a hammer, or an overripe
apricot. It's a heady mixture, that,
glass shards and sweet juice running
all through my veins. You'd think it would
cut. Instead, it flows like a molten
river of lava, shimmering through my skin.
Yesterday, I stood naked in the yard,
steaming from the hot tub, watching the moon
tip its dark side into the empty branches,
a sliver of glimmer, like a fingernail
left to the voodoo of sky.

Beckon what lingers, unspoken, unformed,
and let its newness unfold in you
cool and comfortable as a hand
on a fevered brow. When it comes,
nothing else will matter.

CR&O

Walking the Familiar

for Sage

When the horses hear us coming,
they nicker and whinny
across the white field stubbled
with grass. I stroll with you
along the frozen road, the sky
low and gray as smoke.

As long as we move, you sleep.
The stroller wheels spin you
into their spell. Your lashes
are stars on your cheeks,
small constellation.
What dreams, what lives
remembered, in your slumber?

The river moves whitely in the air.
Mist settles over the hills,
their snow-flocked trees
patterns of light and dark.

It's the month of your birth,
December, month of ending.
The archer shoots his arrows
of fire into the coming night.
Too soon you'll walk on your own
path, no need for me to follow,
then, behind me, wheels
turning over the familiar road.

ಞ

Margaret's Heart

Jake's great blonde sides heave
in the cold of the February barn,
two feet of packed snow
against board-and-batten walls.

Up the road into the farm,
Margaret sleeps against the ticking
of the wood stove down to ash.
Her boots freeze to the floor,

her dreams search out Jake's lost eye,
first clouded, then blind, then gone.
She fingers the velvet dip
between his tobacco-stained mane

and his cheekbone veins,
the socket as smooth and empty
as a toy. Off in the black trees
the sap is slowly climbing

the tall trunks of the maples
sucking sweetness
from the roots to stay alive.
Jake shakes away from the one

dark side of his stall. He snorts
a hot breath into the night,
steam he can see. Soon the light
will crack the sliding door,

Margaret will bring hot mash.
Soon he'll shoulder with Ben,
again, the double yoke,
the dark eye inside the pair

the bright one wide
above the mudcrusted snow.

        ☙❧

Awake at Night

I feel beautiful, young and dying
as the cricket song lifts and calls
and you are far away. No happiness
like this. The maples launch
their spinning seeds, such joy
in the deep air, they twirl down
like toys spun out by boys perched
amongst the leaves.

The lamp shine spreads, honey
around my eyes, and my feet
soles hum to the floor. The hole
inside the core of me rubs its wings,
spins with seeds. I'm not leaving:
rooting, lifting, leafing.

ॐ

My Soul is a Candle That Burned Away the Veil

St. John of the Cross

Everything illuminated becomes this light;
I cannot close my eyes. They become the sky,
become the flame of sheer delight.
The boil of hawks in the kettle of sky.
A horse's face, black bull's black eye,
the piebald cow with her bawl of fright.
Within the hills, the bowl of the valley
cradles the mountains crested in white.
Long though I walk, I will not die.
Everything illuminated becomes this light.

☙❧

Melancholy

Lament for Oso, Washington

We are of this world, oh my people.
Molecule, atom, element,
flesh of the earth, blood of sea,
bone of mountain, breath of wind.
When it shifts and rises, oh my people,
we are its tears, its moans and sighs.
When we build our homes on its flanks,
face with love its serene or roiled
banks, my people, it takes us in,
and when it lifts and slides,
my beloved, my kindred people,
it takes us for its own.

                                      ೞ

Ed's Fence

Two days ago, over the kitchen sink
where the window opens to the east
I heard them sing their celebration song,
their feasting song. It was late,
sun well up, as I fixed the pills
for the old dog wandering
his way toward death.

It caught in my body with precision,
both a chill and the familiar heat:
the yellow ones, the shape shifters,
thieves of hens, hunger afoot.

Hills rise up here making a bowl
of this home. We nestle against
their sheer grassy sides, transplants
from asphalt and concrete. We gaze
upon them, land protected for
what grazes here, cattle and deer.

Between houses, the hens nest
in wood and wire. Their daily range
of lawn and insects timed
to that crepuscular hour
when they turn themselves in
to roost in the dark, lay
when their sire calls in day.

> Once, Coyote came and took a hen
> down the ravine. Song of praise.
> Song of plenty. Once the People
> called him *little brother*
> so sly and light on his feet.

But when they went after Ed's sheep,
he shot one dead and left it to hang
on his fence, skinned but for those feet,
shining white against the sky.

        ☙

Song

Out of the morning's confusion and illness, we walk
into the hills to sit in the early sun.
An eagle sallies overhead, hawks
tie invisible knots in the blue sky.

Tears, and old hard feelings rise
into the autumn air. Deer form
and fade in a copse of trees. The river's drone
drifts above the driveway, a lyre
strung with silver wires of power lines.

Indoors down below is home, a table
and chairs, the window holding the sun in a frame
of leaves. Here on the scrabbled earth, vessels
of bone and flesh, we contain the emptiness
that spills in waves of golden grass.

⊂၄⊃

Paradise, Lost

It is hard to justify gratitude
when hundreds die by fire
in one night. It is hard to justify
gratitude, to feel happy
about anything. Exhaustion
is easier as the sky darkens,
the threat or promise of snow,
of rain that will slide tons
of mud onto what remains.

I cook cranberries. Launder
last week's clothes,
swipe counters and floor
against tomorrow's small
day of thanksgiving.

Last night, I dreamed
my teacher in my arms
in a brown shot-silk dress
burnished with golden hues.
She said, *My skull is the oldest
part of me*, and today
I wonder about that
part born first,
shell over what becomes
memory, knowing, forgetting,
what we call the self.

I'm wandering through the day,
a slight malaise, some bug,
or the weight of loss
that continues to come
after everything we gain.
I'm watching myself fade,

a dream of age. I'm burning
trees for heat, ash gathering
in slow drifts in the grate,
thinking of Paradise, lost
in this age of defeat.

        ☙❧

What I Know of Melancholy

with a nod to Elizabeth Bishop

How water draws it, magnet and salve.
Still water. Moving. Held. How the tide
sweeps it away, leaves the ground wet
and vulnerable to life. How the well
reflects the tunnel-sight of loss. The heart
of the river that beats over rocks that hush
and break. How a woman I did not know,
even her name, went there one winter day
with coffee and pastry and the rifle
that took away the cloying sweetness
and killing pain. I know that river.
I have sat with its shades and reedy stones
to drown my bitterness in its sounds.
It calls forth words for all that I know
I do not know. How it flows, fresh and free
to the ocean it meets, like knowing,
flowing, and flown.

ෆ෩

Spill

Between the blackberry canes
and the deep blue ravine
clouds lick the silver tops
of aspens bare as needles

beneath the October sky.
My mother's voice whirs
the gears of memory:
You sound busy, and *As long*

as you're happy. Later,
exhausted from love's labor
burying the garden for winter
I hear in your impatience
all she also said.

༄

The Weight of Grief

It started with a lump in the throat,
the dog's throat, to be exact. Lying
in the cool grass beneath the spent lilac,
I rubbed her neck and found it. Like a grape,
it rolled between my fingers. *Cyst*, I thought.
At the vet, a week later, it had grown pillow
like and the size of a coin purse. Nothing
to do but love her, which is easy as breathing,
but heavier now. The place in my chest where my heart
hangs beating out its life song
feels like a sack of cement. All the muscles
in my body slack and heavy. Outside,
she lies Sphinx-like between the Mock
Orange and Ponderosa Pine, the best
place to survey her domain. Thunder rumbles,
and somewhere, rain falls on the distant mountains
slaking the onset of drought. Like my tears
gathering in hidden places waiting to fall.

    ☙❧

November Morning

Window shades lighten
as dawn arrives
gray light, chill.
The house is quiet,
still, each of us
in our cocoons.
Soon, the fire must be laid
and lit. Shades lifted
for the short day's light.
My heart is soft
with long life,
with all it knows
about love and loss.
Father, mother;
strangers and friends;
war and famine; disease
and disaster. Yet comes day
with its quiet joy
stirring the blood
and rousing me
to prayer: *May all beings
be free from suffering.*
My riches are safety,
warmth, shelter, food,
health, and love. And knowing
they are not free. They
are not free.

CR&O

Always Forgetting the Little Things

How long the tea has been steeping,
the bitter tannins seeping into the honey
that rises sweetly from the bottom
like puffs of silt released by the stone
of my thinking, its weight dropping slowly
through the water. Ideas that lift
circles concentric as waves of sound,
like the high whistle in my left ear,
the one that catches the wind when I walk
in the hills. Where was I? Sitting here
in the kitchen as the sky changes faces,
gray above the white peaks in the west
like a melancholy mood, Sunday under cloud.
I was thinking about the body, how we know
it as a feeling, a pulse or movement, blood
flowing under the surface of skin, veins,
organs, and the smallest vessels, red lines
of life. Moving such that we can forget
for a moment the intricacy that enlivens us,
time passing in ticks and words and slender
blades of grass picked out against the gloom.

        ☙❧

March Journal

The redwing blackbirds are back,
adding their glossy formality
to the branches of the pine.
By the compost pile,
also black and gleaming
in the new sun, a dead junco
in the rough bunch grass.
The prayer flags are sodden
and rap the window plaintively,
tears of roof melt spattering
the glass. Daily, the snow
draws into itself just as we come
out of ours, the afternoon
light and warm at last.

꽁꽃

Wound

Sometimes, when injury comes
from the world's store of human hurts,
I wail like a child, the child I am yet.

There's a wound inside that never heals.
It waits like something sleeping and hungry,
a bear poked by the stick of tenderness

that roars to life, calls forth my grief.
It's a newness, this deep release
without shame or fear. Love

labored in spasms of awful truth
lasting years. After the sting of skin
torn or burned, the purge of tears,

I rest in my heart newly born.

಄

Sounding

August first and the crickets sing
in the late night breeze that slaps
shades against sills. I'm naked
in the dark, hands slipping over
oiled skin, brushing away cracks
and lines white with dryness.
A mosquito bite on my buttock
burns and itches with persistence
of death. My mother lay so long
abed that her skin wore thin
as hospital sheets, ate and ate
so hungrily at itself. "It won't heal,"
her papery voice said, helpless
and toothless as a baby. Lying here
in my sixty year old hide
the hurt is like a hole of its own,
full of wailing grief, black
as the night sky, unfathomable.

ॐ

Lost Boys

When I was a windy boy and a bit—
No; wait. That's taken and not
so much, you might say, for nursery fit.
Someplace, city or plain, there's an empty lot,
and windy boys and other rags
blow through. Maybe a song, or curse
in the air above their heads like flags
from imagined countries. Nothing worse.

Yet what awaits them, city or plain,
who's got coin, roof, three squares
or nothing, worse. No matter; the stain
still spreads, silent, from empty stares,
someday, when all come home to roost.
Tomorrow, some decades, sometime, all lost.

       CG৪O

Quirks

Blue Hunger

In direct sunlight, the Steller's jay shines
iridescent blue, the same color
as the sharkskin pants my brother wore
in 1968, he and his pals carousing.

The jay hangs precariously from the feeder,
seed spilling wantonly on the ground
scattering lesser birds to the naked trees.

In shade, his pointed cap black as India
ink, a nib that scrawls along the bark
to reach the suet, leaving Morse-like
code in fallen crumbs, his sharp beak
a tool and a weapon.   My brother fell
thirty feet when he was twenty-three
before he fell from grace, hanging
precariously from the family tree.

He broke his thighbone, tore muscle
and skin, thick denim. It broke his fall.
In the hospital room, alone with me one night,
bored and lonely, his hands signed desire
over the other broken part of him: he wanted
me to look, to lift the sheet and see.

Seeds falling in fallow ground remind me—
that and the quick blue slice of hunger.

        ☙

A Sign on the Cascade Highway

Already defunct on first sighting,
weeds parked deep in the lot,
the chain-sawed sign seemed to say
GOOO FOOO, clumsy proclamation
like a mouth too full. GOOO FOOO
you might say cheeks bulging,
eyes alight, just one more
big bite to chew and swallow.
The chainsaw spitting out vowels,
choked on those dental-stopped twin Ds.
The exclamation of all caps
a shout made of what's missing
spaces filled with good wood.

ॐ

With Time

Wind is erasing the hills this morning,
blurring their lines with a white mist
of lifted snow, the northern sky
an imperturbable blue. The turmoil
of air is not its business. I kneel
before Quan Yin; her four arms
hold a lotus, the braided loop of infinity,
and two hands touch in the sign of prayer.

I contemplate the suffering in this world
and ask for relief. It blows like the wind
lifting snow. It sweeps around the Earth
like a silk veil, this exhale. In and out,
breath and wind, darkness and light,
living and dying. It goes on with us
and without. These bones settle on the cushion,
in the body, compressing like the rings of trees,
rooted in the neutral, ever-changing earth.

       ॐ

Waiting

after Ferlinghetti

And I am waiting in the eternal
waiting that trusts what comes
without worrying about what doesn't.
I am waiting for time to reveal
itself in Iris Ribbons waving beneath
the still budding aspen leaves
the soil awakening from winter.

And I am waiting for the dog
to limp across the greening yard
for her gait to steady even as I
am waiting for her legs to fold
and drop her in confusion
at my feet.

      I am waiting
for my own bones to resist
the pull of muscle and joint
the bend the walk the vain
silhouette of not-old-yet.

Waiting for the mystery
within me to bow down
taking waiting away.

        ॐ

Limbs of Love

Last night, in town, a shed exploded
and burnt a house to the ground. Everything was lost
except the cat and the owners and their faith
that things come around right as long as we're alive
and unharmed.   Today, I'm outside
in the ninety-seven-degree heat
limbing the pines that cluster on the south side
of our land, the break between ditch, which burned
last time, and driveway, the final fuel-free
space before our barn. Scorched where fire
climbed the hill, they look like reptiles
and smell like my deepest memories of nature
with their citrusy sap.
            Wielding my lopper
and pine saw—used at Christmas, and now,
in fire season—I slip among them murmuring
words of love. They are good at surrender.

Bark, and green or dry wood yield
and the limbs drop around me like a pyre
or an embrace. One hand on the smooth
bark of branches, and one hand sawing
away what will burn, harm, kill.
Their scent in my sweat like a lover.

    ෬෨

Morning Quail

Feathers pose a question
bobbing blackly on his head,
and all day, he calls Who? Who?
At dawn from the lodgepole
he lobs his query at me,
roused from sleep, dreams
a shadow of wondering
who I am today. In the dim
cocoon, my body curls
into the fetal answer: head,
heart, tail. A fern unfurling.
I am this and that. Between
waking and sleep, a tenderness
opens for his seeking.

ଓଞ

Feeling the Falling

Throughout town, animals are taking care of business.
A family of whitetail deer lucky enough to evade bullets
and arrows daringly dashes across the road ahead of me,
lunch on their minds, fallen apples tantalizing behind
a split-rail fence. Crows break up their meeting beneath
a sprawling pine, black coats shine in the sun. Up
in the hills, the coyotes dig winter dens, and the skunks
have hightailed into burrows around the barn. Things fall.
Leaves, fruit, needles. Snow flocks the high peaks
that ring us round, and clouds glower and billow to lay
down another layer and another. I'm sitting in the late
day silence watching the wind stir the trees and tall grasses.
Watching the sky breathe.

ॐ

At Home on the Range

I don't need their names,
for they are old and familiar
as bones, thrust up from earth

when it was young and wet,
shifting its shape with breath
and blood like birth.

Rows of baleen, they sift light
and rain, smoke and ice, time
pendulous in its golden traces.

They're remote as a mother
unknown. I walk, and walk,
but never get to where they rest

beneath their stony, upturned
breasts. They hover at the edge
of the field, mysteries in mist.

Tumbled, random, and fixed.

༺༻

Emptiness Disguised

Awake at four a.m.
I remember the showers
sailing around Orion's
Belt, late October.
I find my pajamas
shed under the blankets
and stumble into shoes
and down the dark
hall, sliding silently
to avoid the dog.

It's already too late.

The eastern hills rimed
in light, and sky white
with overcast. My eyes
are portals, like camera
lenses adjusting
to the uncertain focus
of air, cloud, distances
nonexistent except
as ideas. The unseen
flares of fiery ice,
remnants of comet,
fly into our space
like snow in the night
blinding against the black,
the way we blink rushing
into it when we drive.

No matter how hard
I look, there's only
emptiness disguised as sight.

Now I Lay Me Down

This is how death may come,
a Sunday night, laying down
a foolish book, my shirt pulled
over my head and tucked
beneath the pillow for morning.
My hair shining gold in the light,
my vanity, my judge in the mirror
soon to be draped, no pendulum
to stop. It's late. Red numbers
flash the hour. I'll close my eyes
and follow my breath, the path
to tomorrow, life or death.

                                                                           ಞ

Quirks of Nature

The male dusky grouse emits
a series of chuffing sounds
that open his cheek feathers
like the round ribbons on medals.

Forsythia blooms in reverse—
flowers followed by leaves.

Each year, the rufous hummingbird
returns first to sip nectar at the window,
a tiny orange menace chirruping fiercely
in a flurry of fiery wings
banishing the hungry.

Sometimes in a woman's body a twin
absorbs its sibling, which grows into a cyst
with hair and teeth waiting to be delivered
by swelling and pain from its mother.

Even I, writing this, am a quirk
of reproduction. One in a million
sperm enlivening the monthly egg.
The singular strand of genes, gender,
rendering me and not another.

       ଔ੪ଓ

Fear

I've heard it said that birds of prey
will take a small pet from a yard.
Somewhere not far from here,
owls nested for years in a dead tree.
Felled by lightning one summer,
inside it held over 200 collars.

At night, I walk my ten-pound dog
around the yard with a leash and headlamp.
Barred owls screech invisibly
from black trees. By day, we never leave
her outside alone as hawks laze
in the autumn sun. Once, recently,
I left her on the patio, the door
to the kitchen open, to look for just a minute
for vinegar to make chutney, plums
drawing flies and sugaring inside.
Stepping out, I shut the door and called
her name expecting the flash of her
in the tall grass or shooting out
from under the deck. One faint bark,
then silence and emptiness that opened
its insatiable maw and roared.

Sky loomed thin as glass.
This familiar land awash in absence.
The shadow bird wrapped itself
around the world. Devoured the bones
and sinew of everything I love.
Comfort. Safety. Home. I ran
the four directions. Wailed into
unanswering air. Faith and trust
dry as dust in my throat. Not even
tears. I fell, stumbling, back

in the house, stunned and clammy with shock.
Peeing behind the door, the dog.

I'd like to say it's gone away, this fear
of death, but love is measured by loss,
nothing safe. We walk beneath its dreamlike
wings, that clasp us inside life.

    ☙❧

Soundscape

Drunk, at a party one summer
on Nova Scotia's South Shore,
my girlfriend at the time said *Someone
needs to tell her hair to shut up!*
Now, it's my own hair that needs
reprimand, cascading over hearing aids
that scritch and scratch every time
I lift it from my nape, that gesture
of luxury. My glasses, likewise,
crash through thickets of hair
like bad scouts lost in the bush.
A hug brings a shrill whistle;
the warning we learned in health
class would accompany heavy petting.
I live now in a cavern with a low
melodic hum of noise like monks
chanting a long, mystical tone,
the sound emptiness holds.

        ೫೦

Coyotes Sing When They Kill

From the hot tub
I see the deer
atop the northern hill
a small herd
big racked buck
in silhouette.
When I look next
they're gone
but the song goes on.
I soak under the gray
shadowed dawn
the world awakening
to its hungers and griefs
their calls companion
to my solitude.
Later, in my room
kneeling in prayer
for this life of love
and loss I hear them
still in the rapture
of communion.
What they take
*Oh Lord of light
and dark* sustains them.
Would that it were so
for us.

Beauty Broken Whole

These mountains you love so much?
Disruptions, ruptures. Once they lay
quiet beneath an inland sea, placid
and flat, soft, smooth sand.
Then the earth heated and shook,
tore at its breast like hands
that broke open fissured ribs
until its molten core poured out.
All a shifting and grinding, thrusting
like trust or truth, like what is buried in
you, dear heart.

        ‗‗‗

Uprising

This morning, mist lifts
in ghosting sheets
from wood and grass
as frost becomes gas.
Up from hay, garlic shoots.
And buds on the still naked
trees glow like a memory
of childhood. High
beyond reach, each
points toward sky
or tomorrow, rich with
color and nascent scent.
There's fresh snow
in the northwest,
peaks beyond peaks
that beckon whitely
in the morning light.
All the greening comes
out of the freeze the way
what we let go rises,
stubborn and free.

☙❧

Picking Raspberries

Not all red are ready. When the light slips
around the black edge of cloud that lights
what hides behind brambles and toothy leaves,
the way they slide from their white insides,
my fingers know ripe from resting. A tender
touch tumbles them, surrendered to the jug on a string
around my neck. Rounding the rows at the garden's
back, fresh deer scat where the mesh has slipped
the post. There's enough for everyone. The fence
lizards, chipmunks in the bird house,
and me, freezing what I will eat come winter.
Every year, we cut them back. And every
year the canes rear up in new places. Like hunger,
diligent, defended, devout.

૱

The Time Between Wolf and Dog

I'm translucent with spaciousness, porous as rain.
Wind whips through open windows, the fine
mesh of screen, like a million points of contact
with the One. Astringent scent of choke-cherry,
bird song, the river roaring, invisible
in the dark ravine. Evening comes with its silver
light. Mountains fade like torn paper
against the sky, a striation of white, blue,
and gray. They notch the view bisected by fence
line and trees, by last year's grasses,
golden and dry, sentinels around what grows
green inside. Everything's slowed to a crawl.
I eat. Drink. Read. Watch. Breathe.
Sun pours blindingly into the empty rooms.
Air with the chill of alpine snow, the cold
of the north falling, sweeping like wolves over flocks
of sheep for slaughter. Cold that pricks the heat
in me to rise to the skin and sing. *Alleluiah.*
Alleluiah. Alleluiah. The dog's sharp bark
at the closed door says *Draw inward,*
O heart, to the fire of your love. God is
near.

☙❧

Country Life

The grey spotted hens
croon their evening prayers.
Rooster's gone. Gone,
too, the layers.
They're together alone
in their eggless days.
Nesting boxes feathered
and bare. All day they scratch
up bugs from the mystery.
Their plucked backs
have healed. Sisterly,
they move as a pair
through table scraps
and autumn grass
day by dawning day
until the farmer comes at last
to bleed their life away.

༺༻

After the Solstice

Chest deep in fresh powder,
clusters of deer eat the tips
of summer's golden grasses,
not waving now. Patient. Roots
sleeping deep under three feet
of snow. Heart-shaped tracks
stitch a trail from hills to house.
Nothing here to threaten them.

Dark-eyed juncoes flit and feed
on scattered millet. Their tiny
formal morning coats and black caps,
their silver waistcoats stretched
over rounded breasts and bellies.

We all fatten in the early dark. Pillowed
and insulated by layers of crystals.
Precious, rare, one of a kind, merged
into this one body, undulate, frozen,
shimmering in the lengthening light.

ஐ

She Writes in Light

Above the slow thaw,
golden strands of grass
arise and dip like threads
loosed from cloth. They stitch
a scrim of notes in the apron
of hill. In this dripping thaw,
everything shifts
back to water. Even those wands
of last summer's light, buried
for months beneath winter
white. Now in tremulous
prayer their blue shadows
bow in diminuendo
of snow.

☙❧

My Mother's Hands

In the photo, they hang oddly from red sweater
cuffs, clutch one of the white paper napkins
she liked to wipe her dripping nose. Caught
this way—each bump and twist of knuckle and bone,
the nails that grew like hooves, so hard to trim—
they look like claws except for the love in her face
as she kisses the baby who meets her lips. It's a shock
to see them dangling from my wrists.

Girl Meets Boy

It wasn't just the bike
although that was a draw.
Mostly, I wanted to be him,
Tommy, like the gun
he also had and shared
as we crawled on our bellies
playing *Combat* around his yard.
Helmet-clad, I was Sergeant Saunders,
his grizzled, blue-eyed face, cigarette,
and the *pop-pop-pop* of the gun.

But the bike—two wheels with no trainers
I had been begging for at home—
he let me ride to prove I could
ride down Pomona Avenue
that summer day, 1963.

Today, it's frame inside frame.

My father with his crew cut and t-shirt
holding the Super 8, and me
flying, grinning, in shorts and fringed,
star-spangled top, around the corner,
then—just like that—spilled sideways
into the street, bewildered,
the film running, recording my failure,
my fall, the first crash of believing
I could do anything I like.

        CR&SO

Night Walk

Full moon. An owl whistles across
the ravine. So many hungers: dark
for light. Bird for meat. The dog sniffs
grass for mice by now inside the house,
the walls, waiting until we sleep to eat
plaster, wood, and wire, flavors in oddments.

Walking in the dark grass, the crunch
of new frost, awareness devours sound,
picks at the moon's reflection on white curtain
in the room above the barn. Still the owl
waits to hunt from her perch, for the rustle
of a meal scuttling in the leaves: mouse,
vole, night walkers parsing the land
for sustenance.
          Breath shines out around me
in the cold fall air, dances with the soft
lunar shine. This body with its jangling joints—
uncertain in the moist night—filled, satisfied.

    ஓஜ

City of Embers

It's night time in the city of embers,
red lights flash in darkness
while up here, it's daylight, sun
streaming whitely into rooms.

In the city of embers, business is brisk.
Amid the gloom, the paramours air
and heat dine on blackened pine.

A voyeur, I peer into the glowing
streets, windows flicker with shadows.
Who's passing within their darkened
rooms? Like a god of plenty, a god of death,
I drop wood into the city of embers,
crushing and igniting, enlightening to flame.

The city of embers embraces its name.

ଓଃ୫ଠ

Mundane

Water glitters.

Last night,
the full moon
lit the sky
like God's eye.

It's May, the river
is high and brown.
White caps light
buried rocks.

It boils along
to meet its lover
five miles down
where they couple
loudly all day long.

Cottonwoods shine,
metallic thread
in the brocade hill
of pines. In the West
the Sawtooths lose
a layer of snow every day.
Cavities of brown
pock the white.

I'm trying to tell you
there's nothing
to write.

ଓଞ୍ଚ

Acknowledgments

I offer my deep gratitude to the editors of these journals for publishing the following poems.

> "On Reading Stafford's 'Is This Feeling about the West Real'" and "Peal," *Shrub-Steppe Poetry Journal*, 2020
>
> "On a Saturday Morning," *Shrub-Steppe Poetry Journal*, 2019
>
> "Lament for Oso," *Washington Poetic Routes*, 2019
>
> "Ed's Fence," *The Florida Review*, 2016
>
> "Awake at Night," and "My Soul is a Candle that Burned away the Veil," *The Cortland Review*, 2012
>
> "Margaret's Heart," *Valparaiso Review*, 2012

My special thanks to the members of the Confluence Poets, particularly Cindy Williams-Gutierrez, Sam Owen, Christine Kendall, and Greg Wright for helping clarify these poems from earlier drafts. To Greg Wright for his friendship and exceptional editing with a clear mind and a kind heart. To the Trillium Awakening Teachers Circle for first guiding and then including me into their midst. And to my beloved, Sugandhi, for love, art, and home.

૱

About the Author

Subhaga Crystal Bacon is a 1995 graduate of the Warren Wilson MFA Program for Writers with a degree in Poetry. Her first book, *Elegy with a Glass of Whiskey*, won the 2003 BOA Editions New Poetry America Prize. Since that time, her work has appeared in a variety of print and online journals. A dramatic shift in consciousness in 2011 brought her into seamless contact with awareness and perception such that she stopped writing for a period of years. Moving to the Methow Valley in 2014 and joining the Confluence Poets reinvigorated her creative process, resulting in many of the poems in this manuscript. She is a teacher in the Trillium Awakening spiritual path and lives and creates in the spacious North Cascade Mountains with her partner, Sugandhi Katharine Barnes, whose painting, *Stella Polaris*, is on the cover.

ॐ

Colophon

Blue Hunger, by Subhaga Crystal Bacon,
was set in Garamond by Methow Press.
The cover design is by Greg Wright.
The cover art, *Stella Polaris*, is by Sugandhi Katharine Barnes.
Manufactured by LightningSource, LaVergne, Tennessee.

CPSIA information can be obtained
at www.ICGtesting.com
Printed in the USA
FSHW021922090620